ABSOLUTE BEGINNERS

Harmonica Songbook

PLAYBACK+
Speed • Pitch • Balance • Loop

To access audio, visit:
www.halleonard.com/mylibrary

Enter Code
7315-6811-5782-7345

ISBN 978-1-5400-5732-7

Copyright © 2023 by HAL LEONARD LLC
International Copyright Secured   All Rights Reserved

Visit Hal Leonard Online at
www.halleonard.com

World headquarters, contact:
Hal Leonard
7777 West Bluemound Road
Milwaukee, WI 53213
Email: info@halleonard.com

In Europe, contact:
Hal Leonard Europe Limited
1 Red Place
London, W1K 6PL
Email: info@halleonardeurope.com

In Australia, contact:
Hal Leonard Australia Pty. Ltd.
4 Lentara Court
Cheltenham, Victoria, 3192 Australia
Email: info@halleonard.com.au

Itsy Bitsy Spider

Traditional

🔊 **Track 1** All songs include online audio for download or streaming. To access the online audio, just head over to **www.halleonard.com/mylibrary** and input the code found on page 1 of this book!

This Old Man

Traditional

Track 2

3. This old man, he played three,
   he played knick-knack on my knee. *(Refrain)*

4. This old man, he played four,
   he played knick-knack on my door. *(Refrain)*

5. This old man, he played five,
   he played knick-knack on my hive. *(Refrain)*

6. This old man, he played six,
   he played knick-knack on my sticks. *(Refrain)*

7. This old man, he played seven,
   he played knick-knack up in heaven. *(Refrain)*

8. This old man, he played eight,
   he played knick-knack on my gate. *(Refrain)*

9. This old man, he played nine,
   he played knick-knack on my spine. *(Refrain)*

10. This old man, he played ten,
    he played knick-knack once again. *(Refrain)*

Long, Long Ago

By Thomas Bayly

Track 3

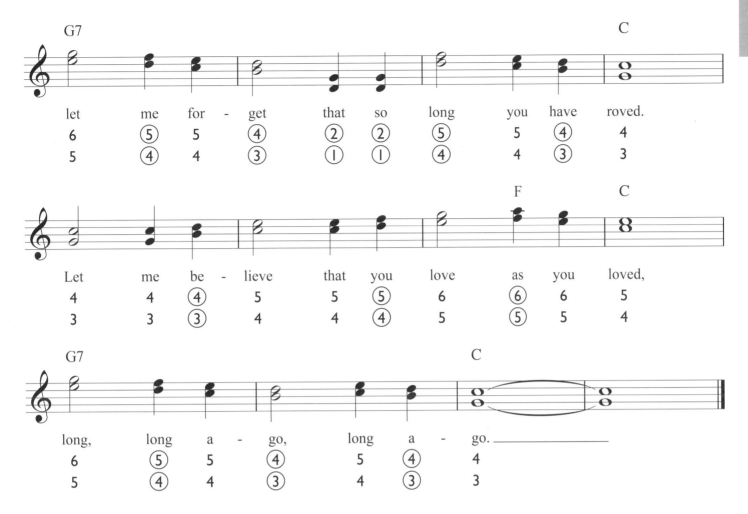

G7   C

let   me   for - get   that   so   long   you   have   roved.
6   ⑤   5   ④   ②   ②   ⑤   5   ④   4
5   ④   4   ③   ①   ①   ④   4   ③   3

                                                                          F   C

Let   me   be - lieve   that   you   love   as   you   loved,
4   4   ④   5   5   ⑤   6   ⑥   6   5
3   3   ③   4   4   ④   5   ⑤   5   4

G7   C

long,   long   a - go,   long   a - go.
6   ⑤   5   ④   5   ④   4
5   ④   4   ③   4   ③   3

Oh! Susanna

Words and Music by Stephen C. Foster

 Track 4

Blowin' in the Wind

Words and Music by Bob Dylan

🔊 **Track 5**

C			F			C						
How	man - y	roads	must	a	man	walk	down	be - fore	you
6	6	6	(6)	(6)	6	6	5	(4)	4	5	6	6

F			G7					C		F	
call	him	a	man?		Yes, 'n'	how	man - y	seas	must	a
(6)	6	(5)	6		5	(5)	6	6	6	(6)	(6)	6

C				F		G7					
white	dove	sail	be - fore	she	sleeps	in	the	sand?		Yes, 'n'
6	5	(4)	4	5	6	6	(5)	5	5	(4)	5	(5)

C			F			C					
how	man - y	times	must	the	can-non - balls	fly	be - fore	they're
6	6	6	(6)	(6)	6	6	6	5	(4)	4	5	6	6

F			G7				F		G7		C
for - ev - er	banned?		The	an - swer, my	friend,	is	blow-in'	in	the
(6)	6	(5)	6		5	(5)	(5)	5	(4)	(4)	5	5	5	(4)

Am			F			G7			C	
wind.	The	an - swer	is	blow-in'	in	the	wind.	
4	5	(5)	(5)	5	(4)	(4)	4	(3)	4

Edelweiss

8

from THE SOUND OF MUSIC
Lyrics by Oscar Hammerstein II
Music by Richard Rodgers

Track 6

You Are My Sunshine

Words and Music by Jimmie Davis

Track 7

Moon River

from the Paramount Picture BREAKFAST AT TIFFANY'S
Words by Johnny Mercer
Music by Henry Mancini

Track 8

I'm an Old Cowhand (from the Rio Grande)

Words and Music by Johnny Mercer

🔊 **Track 9**

I'm an old cow - hand _____ from the Ri - o Grande, _____
6   6   5   4   ④   ④ ④ ⑤ 5   4

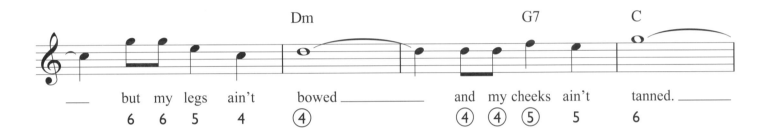

___ but my legs ain't bowed _____ and my cheeks ain't tanned. _____
6   6   5   4   ④   ④ ④ ⑤ 5   6

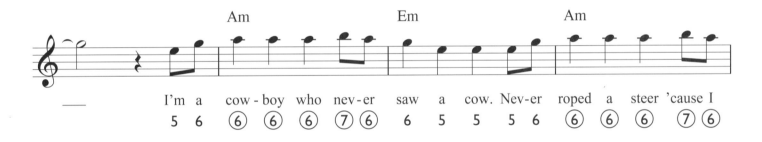

___ I'm a cow - boy who nev-er saw a cow. Nev-er roped a steer 'cause I
5 6 ⑥ ⑥ ⑥ ⑦ ⑥ 6 5 5 5 6 ⑥ ⑥ ⑥ ⑦ ⑥

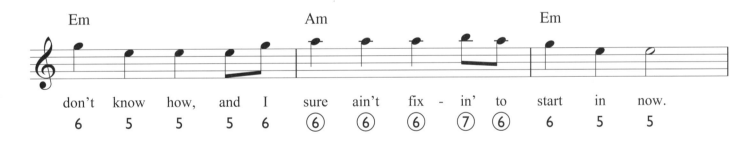

don't know how, and I sure ain't fix - in' to start in now.
6 5 5 5 6 ⑥ ⑥ ⑥ ⑦ ⑥ 6 5 5

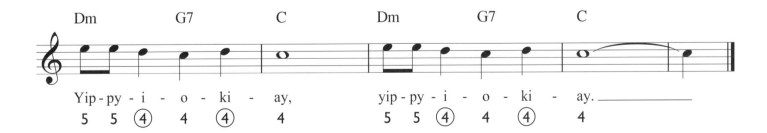

Yip-py - i - o - ki - ay, yip-py - i - o - ki - ay. _____
5 5 ④ 4 ④ 4   5 5 ④ 4 ④ 4

All My Loving

Words and Music by John Lennon and Paul McCartney

Track 10

Ob-La-Di, Ob-La-Da

Words and Music by John Lennon and Paul McCartney

 Track 11

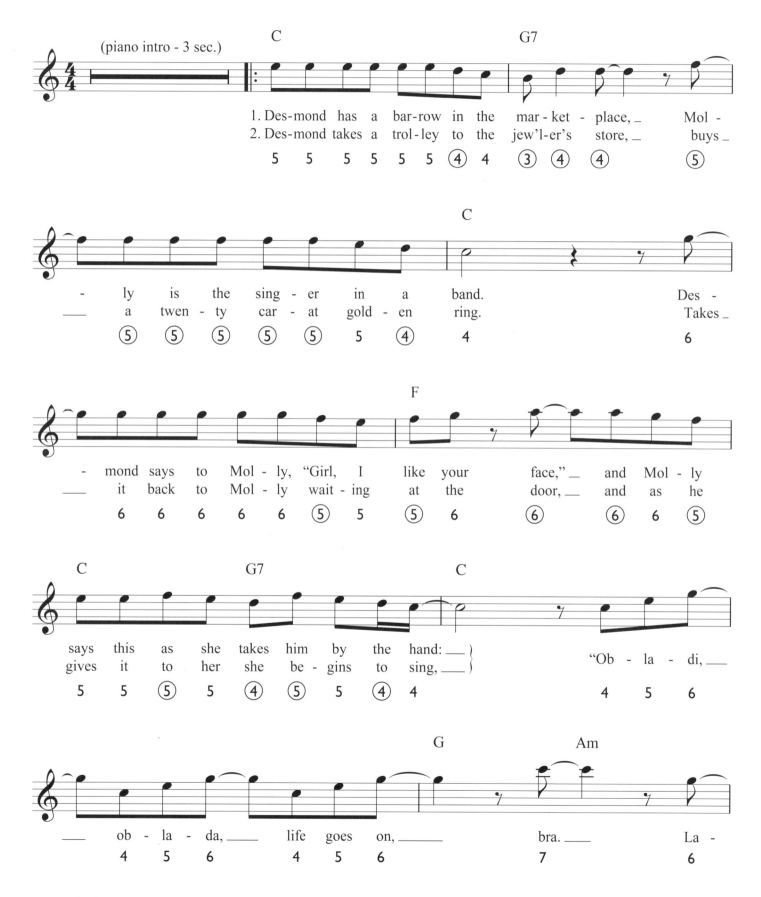

Your Cheatin' Heart

Words and Music by Hank Williams

Track 12

Every Breath You Take

Music and Lyrics by Sting

 Track 13

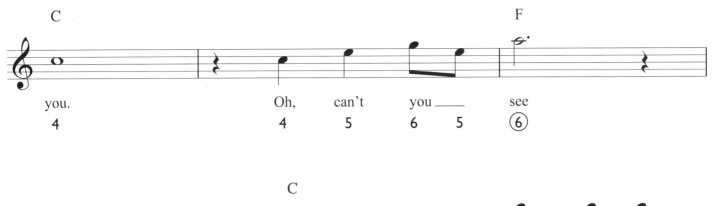

C   F

you.   Oh,   can't   you ___   see

4   4   5   6   5   ⑥

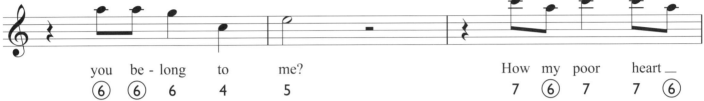

C

you   be - long   to   me?   How   my   poor   heart ___

⑥   ⑥   6   4   5   7   ⑥   7   7   ⑥

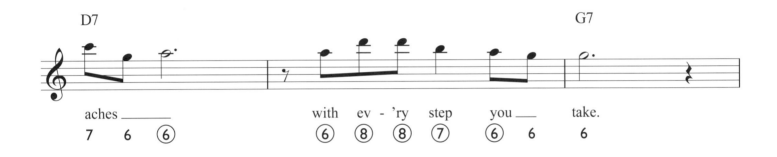

D7   G7

aches ___   with   ev - 'ry   step   you ___   take.

7   6   ⑥   ⑥   ⑧   ⑧   ⑦   ⑥   6   6

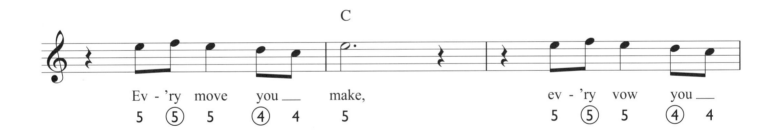

C

Ev - 'ry   move   you ___   make,   ev - 'ry   vow   you ___

5   ⑤   5   ④   4   5   5   ⑤   5   ④   4

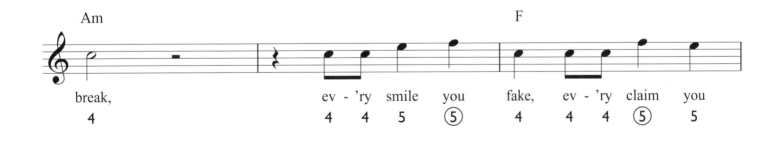

Am   F

break,   ev - 'ry   smile   you   fake,   ev - 'ry   claim   you

4   4   4   5   ⑤   4   4   4   ⑤   5

Begin fade

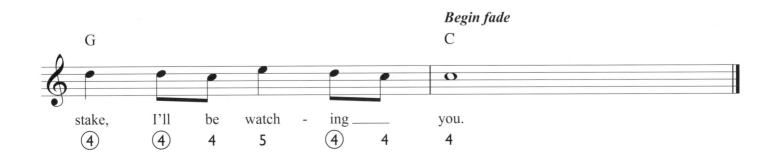

G   C

stake,   I'll   be   watch - ing ___   you.

④   ④   4   5   ④   4   4

It's a Small World

from Disney Parks' "it's a small world" attraction
Words and Music by Richard M. Sherman and Robert B. Sherman

Track 14

Ring of Fire

Words and Music by Merle Kilgore and June Carter

 Track 15